ARRIVALS AND DEPARTURES

Rogelio Martinez

BROADWAY PLAY PUBLISHING INC
New York
www.broadwayplaypublishing.com
info@broadwayplaypublishing.com

First printing: December 2008
Second printing: April 2013
I S B N: 978-0-88145-427-7

Book design: Marie Donovan
Typeface: Palatino

ARRIVALS AND DEPARTURES was presented in 2004 as part of the first annual Summer Play Festival.

CHARACTERS & SETTING

CELIN, *a novelist, thirties*
MAYITO, *a novelist, thirties, his older brother*
MARGARITA, *thirties, their sister*

Place: Sancti-Spiritus, Cuba

Time: 1985

ACT ONE

Scene One

(Sancti-Spiritus, Cuba. 1985)

(A study. No one is on stage yet. An old cherry wood desk. On it there is a Remington typewriter, a handful of papers, reading glasses, and an old Tiffany lamp. A single café cup rests empty next to the typewriter. Several green volumes lie closed near the edge of the desk. There is a sturdy wooden chair behind the desk.)

(CELIN enters. He looks around and picks up a book, gently. After a moment he closes it, accidentally unsettling dust that has remained undisturbed for decades.)

(Outside a band is heard playing a very somber version of the Internationale.*)*

(MARGARITA enters.)

MARGARITA: There you are. I've been looking all over for you.

CELIN: You told them I was here!

MARGARITA: Who?

CELIN: All of them—the whole town. They've sent a marching band to welcome me.

MARGARITA: No.

CELIN: Listen. That's love just pouring out of them.

MARGARITA: I don't—

CELIN: They love me.

MARGARITA: They came around this morning too. Just before you got here.

CELIN: And after all these years—I was afraid, you know. I was afraid they'd forgotten me. After all these years—

MARGARITA: Celin.

CELIN: You're right. You're right. I have to do something for them—acknowledge them somehow. I have just the thing! An excerpt from my new novel. It's about capitalism, the destructive force that haunts a market economy—it's a thriller but of high literary value. Did you leave my bags in the hallway? *(He goes to exit.)*

MARGARITA: That band is not for you.

CELIN: Of course it is.

MARGARITA: No. It isn't.

CELIN: How do you know?

MARGARITA: It's a funeral march. Chernenko died today.

CELIN: Chernenko—Chernenko...

MARGARITA: Yes! Chernenko.

CELIN: That isn't...it isn't for me?

MARGARITA: Well, if he hadn't died I'm sure—

CELIN: They're not playing for me?

MARGARITA: No.

CELIN: I thought I meant something to this town.

MARGARITA: You do.

CELIN: Do they know I lived here? Do those people out there even know who I am?

MARGARITA: I'm sure they do. It's just you picked the wrong day.

CELIN: How many of them have died in the past two and a half years?

MARGARITA: What?

CELIN: First Brezhnev. Then Andropov. Now Chernenko. When a Soviet Secretary General dies it's no longer—well no one cares! No. No. No. This is no good. I thought there would at least be a representative, someone from the town, the mayor—

MARGARITA: Will you listen to yourself. What do you care who they're playing for? This isn't your home anymore.

CELIN: Of course it is.

MARGARITA: Five years, Celin.

CELIN: Five years?

MARGARITA: Yes.

CELIN: Has it been five years?

MARGARITA: Almost six.

CELIN: I couldn't just stop what I was doing to come here.

MARGARITA: You don't have to—

CELIN: There were things.... I don't know. I suppose it was wrong—all wrong.... I want you to know that this place, this house, you...not a day goes by when I don't think about home. Watch! *(He takes out a handkerchief.)*

MARGARITA: What are you doing?

(CELIN walks around the room using the handkerchief as a blindfold.)

CELIN: This was Papi's room.

MARGARITA: Celin.

CELIN: We were never allowed in here while he was working but that didn't stop me. I wasn't afraid of him. I'd sneak in when he was working. And I'd sit and watch him work. Mostly hear him—his typing away and mumbling to himself, but every once in a while I'd look out from behind the chair...this chair.

MARGARITA: Take that off—

CELIN: No. I'll prove to you if I have to—

MARGARITA: You have nothing to prove to me.

CELIN: That I remember everything about this room—this house. Now let go.

(MARGARITA does. CELIN bumps into the desk.)

MARGARITA: Are you satisfied?

CELIN: I won't stop until I can walk around the house without hurting myself. The house is the same. You haven't moved the— *(He bumps into a chair.)*

MARGARITA: No.

CELIN: That wasn't always there. It was in another part—

MARGARITA: You just don't remember.

CELIN: Stop it.

MARGARITA: What?

CELIN: Stop laughing at me. This is important.

MARGARITA: What?

CELIN: Remembering where I used to live. I don't want to ever forget. *(He crashes again.)*

MARGARITA: You have two perfectly good eyes.

CELIN: They deceive me.

MARGARITA: Don't go there—

(CELIN *hits a wall and sits down on the floor.*)

CELIN: Our brother can't know—

MARGARITA: What?

CELIN: That I can't remember where anything is.

MARGARITA: Why would he care?

CELIN: Papi told me writers remember everything. Like elephants. He'd sit and write remembering every prick and punch someone threw his way— every hurtful glance, every sign of doubt. He saw writing as a way of remembering and responding.

MARGARITA: That's not writing.

CELIN: What is it then?

MARGARITA: Hostility maybe.

CELIN: He was very successful.

MARGARITA: He was very hostile. Now take that off.

CELIN: When is Mayito getting here?

MARGARITA: Take that off. Now. You're a baby.

CELIN: Your baby brother.

MARGARITA: No. A baby.

(CELIN *takes off the handkerchief.*)

CELIN: I'm a failure.

MARGARITA: No. You're not.

CELIN: Yes. I am.

MARGARITA: Fine. You are.

CELIN: Really? What makes you say that?

MARGARITA: I don't have time for this today.

CELIN: Why? Is it because Mayito is returning? Mayito the New Yorker—the sensation. Is that what you think? I have worked—I am equally—if not more—

MARGARITA: What?

CELIN: Successful.

MARGARITA: Whatever happens—

CELIN: Nothing is going to happen.

MARGARITA: I don't want you fighting.

CELIN: I promise you I'll be the good little boy you remember.

MARGARITA: You were never good.

CELIN: Our brother was worse.

MARGARITA: You were both little terrors.

CELIN: I was only following orders. I'm sorry if we hurt you.

MARGARITA: If?

CELIN: I'm sorry. *(Pause)* It's wonderful—what you've done—how you've kept this house.... It's almost as if nothing's changed.

MARGARITA: Nothing really has. I had to get both of your rooms ready. That's not an easy task. To bring things forgotten and long used up back to life.

CELIN: For me it's always alive.

MARGARITA: That's because you didn't stay behind. Everything here died long ago. Now why don't I show you the other rooms. *(She moves to exit.)*

CELIN: Shouldn't our brother be here by now?

MARGARITA: I'm sure he'll be here soon.

CELIN: He's late—and you know why? He wants to make an entrance. That boy hasn't changed.

MARGARITA: He's a man now. Whether you care to admit it or not, we've all changed. Anyway, he probably got stuck somewhere. He's coming all the way from New York. Did you know he's already flown around the world—once he even went on the Concorde. I don't know how he does it. I'm so afraid of flying.

CELIN: You're afraid of everything. Even men.

MARGARITA: Why do you say that?

CELIN: I expected—you are of that age.

MARGARITA: What?

CELIN: You should be married. Or at the very least, you should be wrecking some other woman's marriage.

MARGARITA: I have other interests.

CELIN: Like what?

MARGARITA: Things I like to do.

CELIN: What?

MARGARITA: It doesn't matter.

CELIN: I'd like to know.

MARGARITA: Why now? Why take an interest in my life now?

CELIN: That's unfair.

MARGARITA: I'm sorry.

CELIN: I have—you're always on my mind.

MARGARITA: Where do you think our brother will go to first?

CELIN: Isn't he coming straight here?

MARGARITA: No. No. When he goes wandering about. What do you think he'll want most to see.

CELIN: El Teatro Principal.

MARGARITA: I was afraid of that.

CELIN: It was his favorite movie theater.

MARGARITA: It's now the People's Movie House.
Or it was until last week.

CELIN: What happened?

MARGARITA: It burned down.

CELIN: It did?

MARGARITA: Nothing left of it. Except they found an
old reel of a movie. Clint Eastwood. *The Good, the Bad
and the Ugly*. Maybe Mayito knows him.

CELIN: Clint Eastwood?

MARGARITA: Our brother knows a lot of famous people.

CELIN: I know the mayor of La Habana.

MARGARITA: I love Westerns. There's justice in them.

CELIN: Movies.

MARGARITA: Why don't you write a movie? A western.

CELIN: Life is not black and white.

MARGARITA: Shoot it in color.

CELIN: No. What I meant— No more movie theatre?

MARGARITA: I lost my job. I was the projectionist there.

CELIN: Were you there the day of the fire?

MARGARITA: I'm not afraid of fire.

CELIN: You should be.

MARGARITA: It's not like you can't put it out. Anger.

CELIN: What about it?

MARGARITA: Anger I would fear.

(Pause)

CELIN: He has other places he can go.

MARGARITA: What?

CELIN: Why didn't you meet him at the airport?

MARGARITA: I don't like airports.

CELIN: Margarita, he's never come home.

MARGARITA: So?

CELIN: What I'm trying to say is that he'll leave again. There's no question he will.

MARGARITA: I know that. So will you.

CELIN: I've never really left you. Yes. I live in La Habana. I got married—as a man my age must, but I've never left you.

MARGARITA: Celin.

CELIN: Five years is not forever.

MARGARITA: Six.

CELIN: Six. Whatever.

MARGARITA: Seven. I lied.

CELIN: I'm not sure it's been that long.

MARGARITA: You're a little boy—no concept of time. Maybe that's why you look the way you look.

CELIN: What?

MARGARITA: Like a kid. I have to dye my hair.

CELIN: You do?

(CELIN starts messing with MARGARITA's hair.)

MARGARITA: Hey!

CELIN: Oh, wow. You've gone gray.

MARGARITA: Don't you dare put that in one of your books.

CELIN: If you're good to me—

MARGARITA: You don't have one gray hair yet. What's your secret?

CELIN: Success.

(Suddenly, MARGARITA hugs CELIN.)

MARGARITA: It's good to have you back.

CELIN: Why don't you ever come visit?

MARGARITA: I'd get lost in La Habana.

CELIN: My wife will show you around. I have maps—

MARGARITA: Not that kind of lost.

CELIN: Has our brother asked you to go live with him in New York?

MARGARITA: Yes.

CELIN: Why haven't you?

MARGARITA: And live among whores.

CELIN: What?

MARGARITA: You won't believe this but things are really bad in New York. Apparently everyone is a whore.

CELIN: How do you know that?

MARGARITA: In his letters he writes to me that his editor, his publisher, they're both whores. It's the only way to make a living there.

CELIN: How does our brother do it?

MARGARITA: I refuse to ask him.

CELIN: You think—

MARGARITA: I'm afraid our brother is a writer and a whore.

(The band is heard again.)

CELIN: Oh, God, there they go again. Are you sure the town remembers me?

MARGARITA: Yes.

CELIN: Why isn't this house a museum?

MARGARITA: A museum?

CELIN: I just thought—this is where I wrote my first story. My first success.

MARGARITA: It's already a museum. For you to remember who you are. And that gets very tiring after a while. If I want to change something—if there's something I want to do to the house, I stop myself because I know that if I do you'll never come back.

CELIN: That's not true.

MARGARITA: It isn't?

CELIN: And really what I want—what I deserve is an official museum with my first typewriter, all my books, my letters—why am I back if they don't care?

MARGARITA: You're not back for them.

CELIN: Tell them to go away. I'm trying to work.

MARGARITA: Celin.

CELIN: Tell them I'm here. They know who I am. They've all read my books. Tell them to shut up.

MARGARITA: It's for Chernenko.

CELIN: For Brezhnev. Andropov. Chernenko. Who cares?

MARGARITA: A lot of us do. At least that's what I get from reading your books. Or are they all lies?

CELIN: I'm sorry. You're sad.

MARGARITA: It's the end of something.

CELIN: What?

MARGARITA: I don't know.

(MARGARITA *exits. The band plays.*)

(CELIN *puts on the handkerchief. He tries to walk around the room. After a moment, the band is no longer heard.* MAYITO *enters. Obviously* CELIN *can't see him.*)

MAYITO: Where is the ass?

CELIN: What?

MAYITO: Pin the tail on the donkey.

CELIN: Mayito!

MAYITO: You're still playing games.

(CELIN *takes off his handkerchief.*)

(*Pause*)

MAYITO: You look young.

CELIN: So do you.

MAYITO: Kids.

CELIN: Right.

MAYITO: Peter Pan. Remember?

CELIN: What?

MAYITO: Games. I was Peter Pan and you were Wendy.

CELIN: I was *never* Wendy.

MAYITO: Of course you were. We used to stick you in that yellow dress.

CELIN: What dress?

MAYITO: That didn't do anything to you—you're not...

CELIN: Wendy? No.

MAYITO: Celin in the morning and Wendy at night.

CELIN: I was never Wendy.

MAYITO: You don't remember.

CELIN: No. It just didn't happen that way. Our sister was Wendy. I was one of the Lost Boys.

MAYITO: Are you still lost?

CELIN: I'm not the one who wandered so far from home.

(Pause)

MAYITO: Is she here?

CELIN: Just went outside for a moment. *(Pause)* I can't believe.

MAYITO: Yes.

CELIN: I thought about what I would say—I reread my books. All of them. Looking for moments where brothers—nothing. They don't have much to say— brothers. In my books that is...

MAYITO: I wrote notes to myself. Things we could talk about in case— *(Long silence)* My suit. I hope it fits you. I'm planning to leave it with you.

CELIN: I don't need it.

MAYITO: I brought you an entire wardrobe.

CELIN: I have closets full of clothes.

MAYITO: Sorry to tell you this but leisure suits and plaid went out of style a few years ago.

(CELIN is slightly embarrassed by this. MAYITO picks up on this and backs off.)

MAYITO: What were you doing with the handkerchief?

CELIN: Nothing.

MAYITO: You always loved games.

CELIN: I was a happy kid?

MAYITO: Yes.

CELIN: And you were a bully. I won't let you beat me up this time.

MAYITO: Oh, but you must let me have some fun.

(MARGARITA *enters.*)

MARGARITA: Mayito!

(MARGARITA *and* MAYITO *hug.*)

MARGARITA: Let me look at you. You look—

CELIN: Like a fat imperialist pig.

MARGARITA: Now stop it. Oh, God. You are here— finally! Finally here. What can I say! (*She hugs him.*) Let's get you out of these clothes.

CELIN: What?

MARGARITA: I'll run you a bath. I can't believe you're here. Wait. Your face. Your hands. Let me touch you finally.

MAYITO: Okay. Okay. I'm going to be here for a few days.

MARGARITA: Turn around.

MAYITO: Why?

MARGARITA: I want to see all of you.

(MAYITO *turns around.*)

CELIN: That's what I remember. At the airport. You didn't even turn around when you got to the gate.

MAYITO: I was afraid you weren't going to be there.

MARGARITA: No fighting, okay?

MAYITO: That's all right.

MARGARITA: How did you get in? I was standing in front of the house.

MAYITO: I snuck in through the back.

MARGARITA: Why?

MAYITO: Twenty-five years ago—my God, twenty five years. Wow. It sounds like another life.

CELIN: It is.

MAYITO: Anyway, I left through that back door. I thought it only fitting to return the same way.

(MARGARITA *hugs him again.*)

MARGARITA: I told friends you were coming. They all want to see you.

MAYITO: Do they?

MARGARITA: They know so much about you through me. It's as if you grew up here.

CELIN: Do they know about me?

MARGARITA: Of course, Celin, you're famous.

MAYITO: So am I.

CELIN: Not here. What you are over there means nothing here.

MAYITO: I brought my books with me.

MARGARITA: I can't read English.

MAYITO: You do. Maybe you can—

CELIN: If I have the time.

MAYITO: Of course.

CELIN: I'm a very busy man.

MAYITO: I understand.

CELIN: I haven't been home myself in a few years.

MARGARITA: Home. I love saying that word. All of us home.

CELIN: And what about Papi? Did you bring him back?

MAYITO: Kicking and screaming. He didn't want to come.

CELIN: He didn't?

MAYITO: It wasn't his choice though, was it? (*He starts to exit but in fact he's walking over to where his luggage is. He takes out a wooden box with ashes.*)

MAYITO: He wanted them left at some airport.

MARGARITA: He told you that?

MAYITO: Left it on a note. After twenty five years over there he was convinced he still hadn't arrived. That he was waiting for a connecting flight that would take him somewhere—to another life I suppose. He hated his life. I left half of him at the airport.

MARGARITA: He was always only half here.

CELIN: That's half?

MAYITO: More or less. One of the officials at the airport thought it was drugs. He put a pinch on his tongue, spit him right back out. Papi always had that kind of effect on people.

CELIN: I don't get it. (*He takes the ashes.*)

MAYITO: What?

CELIN: How one moment you can have someone there all flesh and blood, the next ashes.

MARGARITA: Actually it takes hours. They put him in this box and stick him in an oven—

CELIN: I wasn't really asking.

MAYITO: There are still some small bones. There. You see? That's what convinced them I was telling the truth

MARGARITA: Oh, that always happens with fire. It leaves behind footprints, clues....

MAYITO: I feel so powerful standing over him like this. I can hold him in one hand. What son can say that?

(MARGARITA *has been looking at the ashes.*)

MARGARITA: That's odd.

MAYITO: What?

MARGARITA: That bone. His nose—so easy to break when you're alive but can't turn it into ashes. He had a cute nose.

CELIN: Just like mine.

MARGARITA: No. Slightly more aristocratic than yours.

MAYITO: Like mine.

MARGARITA: Like mine. Look at yours in the mirror and then look at mine.

(CELIN *takes the ashes.*)

CELIN: Should we say something?

MAYITO: Like what?

MARGARITA: Let me hold him. *(She takes them.)*

CELIN: I don't know. We're standing over half his body. I feel we should say something.

MARGARITA: That we all—

CELIN: We're both writers after all. *(He takes them.)*

MAYITO: All right. I'll say something. *(He tries to take them.)*

CELIN: Maybe I should be the one.

MAYITO: I'm the oldest.

CELIN: I've been writing longer.

MAYITO: What are you talking about. I was published at sixteen.

CELIN: In *Popular Mechanics*—some letter to the editor. Oh, please.

(MARGARITA *grabs the ashes.*)

CELIN: Careful.

MAYITO: The oldest boy should say something. That would be me.

CELIN: Forget it.

MARGARITA: Just that we loved you.

CELIN: Yes.

(MAYITO *takes them.*)

MAYITO: That I loved you more than anything.

(CELIN *tries to take them. They struggle.*)

CELIN: We all loved him.

MAYITO: I brought him home. I wanted to bring him home to you because you always thought I took him away.

(MARGARITA *exits with the ashes.*)

MAYITO: Where is she going?

CELIN: I don't know.

(*They watch her walk away. After a moment...*)

MAYITO: I'm happy to see you.

CELIN: So am I.

(MAYITO *wanders around the desk.*)

MAYITO: His old Remington—with ribbon and everything.

CELIN: I haven't touched it.

MAYITO: And his ten volume history of Cuba.

CELIN: Yes.

MAYITO: Why?

CELIN: What?

MAYITO: Ten volumes. Of Cuba. One volume—
two maybe. But ten? It's Cuba!

CELIN: Is there something—

MAYITO: Nothing has changed.

CELIN: What's wrong?

(Pause)

MAYITO: I was waiting for her to—. I lied, Celin.
Papi didn't die in his sleep.

(Pause)

CELIN: He didn't?

MAYITO: No.

CELIN: Like Mami?

MAYITO: Yes.

CELIN: I suppose they had more in common than they'd
ever admit. Were you the one who found him?

MAYITO: A neighbor called. By the time I got there the
cops—he'd been dead for a while. I couldn't be in the
room for more than a minute. Listen I don't want her
to know.

CELIN: No. Of course not.

MAYITO: I wouldn't want to upset her. It might send
her off in the wrong direction.

CELIN: She's already headed that way.

(MARGARITA *enters.*)

MARGARITA: What's going on?

CELIN: Nothing. We were just....

MAYITO: What did you do with the ashes?

MARGARITA: I put them under the front step. Every day I'll walk lightly over him—just to let him know I'm here.

(A bell is heard off stage.)

MAYITO: What's that?

MARGARITA: Felipe from next door. He's coming around for Señor Alberto's food. If Señor Alberto doesn't eat by two he gets very grumpy.

MAYITO: Who are these people?

MARGARITA: Señor Alberto is a pig.

MAYITO: Huh?

MARGARITA: Felipe comes around after lunch and collects the leftovers. Señor Alberto is so healthy, so strong, adorable. I'll take you over to meet him. You'll fall in love. Now are you ready to eat? I'm keeping the food warm on the stove.

MAYITO: Yes.

MARGARITA: I'll tell Felipe to come back and I'll go set out lunch.

MAYITO: Do you need help?

MARGARITA: You in the kitchen? Last time you did that you almost burned the whole place down.

MAYITO: I don't remember.

CELIN: There isn't much you do remember.

MAYITO: Why don't I take a bath first.

MARGARITA: Let me get it ready.

MAYITO: Thank you. I can do it—

MARGARITA: Can I take that to your room?

MAYITO: My room?

MARGARITA: Yes.

MAYITO: Is it still my room?

MARGARITA: Nothing has changed. I left it just the way it was.

MAYITO: Messy?

MARGARITA: Well, no. I made the bed and picked up all the toys. I dusted all over—even under the dresser.

MAYITO: Why did you do that?

MARGARITA: I thought—

MAYITO: Where are my toys?

MARGARITA: I gave them away.

MAYITO: I want you to go to all the kids in the neighborhood and get them back.

MARGARITA: They're grown men by now.

(Pause)

MAYITO: Oh. Right. Then it's not how I left it.

MARGARITA: No. Not exactly-

MAYITO: Like this photo. *(He takes out a photograph.)* Look at me. Ten years old. My last photo here. My room.

MARGARITA: You've been looking at that picture far too long for things here to make you happy. *(She exits.)*

MAYITO: She's right you know.

CELIN: What?

MAYITO: I want it all to be like this.

(The band is heard again.)

MAYITO: What's that?

CELIN: They've been playing all day—

MAYITO: Really.

CELIN: To welcome *me* home.

MAYITO: What?

CELIN: The town is going crazy. Joy really. I've brought joy home. I've been away three years and even that's too long for them. Their favorite son. They love me. Do you hear that?

MAYITO: Celin.

CELIN: Just listen.

MAYITO: Are you sure it's not...

CELIN: What?

MAYITO: For us? I do have—

CELIN: For you?

MAYITO: For both of us? I've done very well on my own.

CELIN: I'm the one responsible for that. Now listen.

MAYITO: They knew I was coming home.

CELIN: You're lucky they allowed you to come back at all. You had to sneak in through the back door, but I have a band welcoming me home. Shh. Listen. Just listen.

MAYITO: But—

CELIN: Listen!

(The band plays.)

(Blackout)

Scene Two

(The next day)

(Early morning. A rooster is heard. MAYITO *is typing at his father's typewriter.* CELIN *enters in pajamas.)*

CELIN: Do you have any idea what time it is?

MAYITO: The strangest thing happened this morning. There, on the floor, next to my bed a frog. Not just a frog. This thing was huge. There it was. Out of some odd, twisted fairy tale—croaking. Kiss me. Kiss me. Would you believe that?

CELIN: You understood this...the frog?

MAYITO: Yes.

CELIN: I thought the only language you understood was money.

*(*MAYITO *croaks again, angrily.)*

CELIN: Stop that. It's seven in the morning.

MAYITO: I got on my knees and was—I mean, it sounds ridiculous now but I was about to give it a great, big wet one when it jumped clear over my head and out into the hallway. I ran after it but it was gone.

CELIN: It happens to everyone who returns.

MAYITO: It does?

CELIN: The moment all of you get here you drop to your knees and start kissing everything—your eyes to the ground because if you were to look up—even for a moment—you'd see everything has changed.

(Pause)

MAYITO: Enough. I'm trying to work.

CELIN: That kind of reality frightens you, doesn't it?

MAYITO: I want to be alone.

CELIN: Too late for that. Your typing woke me up.

MAYITO: I get going early.

CELIN: Why are you using his typewriter?

MAYITO: I don't think he'll mind, do you?

CELIN: No one has used that thing since he left.

MAYITO: It still works.

CELIN: Not your right to use it.

MAYITO: Oh, yeah.

CELIN: He didn't give you permission.

MAYITO: You got to be kidding me. *(He returns to working.)*

CELIN: Can I see?

MAYITO: What?

CELIN: What you wrote.

MAYITO: Nothing really—you can look at that one.

CELIN: This is a list of things you want to do while you're here.

MAYITO: Take this one.

CELIN: You haven't written anything here.

MAYITO: Look; you mind.

(CELIN goes to grab the paper that MAYITO has been typing on.)

MAYITO: Hey! Not this one.

CELIN: No?

(MAYITO folds his arm over the typewriter and what he's been writing—very territorial.)

MAYITO: I never let anyone - not at this point.

CELIN: Something new?

MAYITO: Yes.

(MARGARITA *enters.*)

MARGARITA: Good morning.

CELIN: I thought you were in bed.

MARGARITA: I went to get bread early this morning.

MAYITO: I was up. I didn't hear you.

MARGARITA: Very early this morning.

CELIN: What's this on your face? It's black.

MARGARITA: I must have got my face dirty when I fell.

MAYITO: You fell?

MARGARITA: That's what I said. I'm all right.

MAYITO: It doesn't look like dirt.

CELIN: Where is it?

MARGARITA: What?

CELIN: The bread.

MARGARITA: It hadn't arrived.

MAYITO: Are you sure you're all right?

MARGARITA: I was early. I thought it was seven but it was only...what's wrong?

CELIN: Is that all that happened?

MARGARITA: You boys and your imagination. I'll go make café.

MAYITO: Margarita—

MARGARITA: I'm all right.

(MARGARITA *exits.* MAYITO *tries to get back to work.*)

CELIN: Our sister is a little—

MAYITO: What?

CELIN: Her whole life is here. We both left but Margarita never even made it out of the house.

MAYITO: Crazy.

CELIN: Trapped.

MAYITO: Where was she?

CELIN: I don't know.

MAYITO: I've asked her to come live with me.

CELIN: I have too.

MAYITO: Then she's not trapped.

CELIN: Crazy.

MAYITO: It's so easy to go crazy nowadays. *(He sits back down at the typewriter.)*

CELIN: You know a thing or two about it?

MAYITO: Yes.

CELIN: Are you trying to go back to work?

MAYITO: That was the intention.

CELIN: Have some café with us and then—

MAYITO: I think I have something.

CELIN: It'll be there later. It always is.

MAYITO: Not always.

(MAYITO works. CELIN stares at him.)

(After a moment CELIN sings Guantanamera *under his breath.)*

CELIN: *Guantanamera, guajira guantanamera*
Yo soy un hombre sincero
De donde crece la palma

Y antes de morirme quiero
Echar mis versos del alma

MAYITO: *Stop.*

CELIN: Was I doing anything?

MAYITO: You were.

CELIN: Sorry. Look why don't you wait for the café.

MAYITO: It's just I got this thing now—

CELIN: Come on.

(Pause)

MAYITO: All right.

(Short pause)

CELIN: How does it feel?

MAYITO: What?

CELIN: Working on the old man's typewriter.

MAYITO: The keys are heavy, stubborn, full of resistance. It's like a boxing match—every letter is a punch.

CELIN: Do you like it?

MAYITO: No.

CELIN: You like things to come easy.

MAYITO: I didn't say that.

(Pause)

CELIN: You don't have anything to say to me?

MAYITO: Do you? *(Pause)* How is your wife?

CELIN: She's having an affair.

MAYITO: Are you sure?

CELIN: Am I sure? I have live sound, phone calls—wire tapping—photographs, surveillance video, but

I've never caught her in the act so there's some room for doubt.

MAYITO: You follow her around?

CELIN: I don't have to. I have friends who do that.

MAYITO: Friends as in...

CELIN: Friends as in what?

MAYITO: Government people, I mean. Is that right? Government people?

CELIN: Maybe.

MAYITO: What are you going to do about it?

CELIN: I've put it in their hands. It's up to them now.

MAYITO: What do you mean it's in their hands? Whose hands?

CELIN: I can't say.

MAYITO: What the fuck are you talking about?

CELIN: My wife is a traitor.

MAYITO: Huh?

CELIN: I told them she was reading Ayn Rand. Not a very popular author around here.

MAYITO: Is that a crime?

CELIN: Fucking around behind my back is.

MAYITO: I'm kind of confused now.

CELIN: One hand washes the other.

MAYITO: Look; go see a marriage counselor before you end up doing—

CELIN: What's that?

MAYITO: A professional who talks you out of doing something stupid.

CELIN: That's an interesting job.

(MARGARITA *enters with the café.*)

MARGARITA: There was a frog in my kitchen.

CELIN: Really? Maybe he knows something about it.

(MAYITO *is popping a few pills.*)

MARGARITA: I chased it with the broom.

(CELIN *helps* MARGARITA *with the café.*)

CELIN: Let me take that.

MARGARITA: I caught it and brought it outside.

MAYITO: When we were kids there was one that lived under my bed. Do you think it's still there?

MARGARITA: From when you were a kid?

MAYITO: Yes.

(MARGARITA *shakes her head no.*)

MAYITO: Fuck. (*He pops a few more pills.*)

MARGARITA: What are you taking?

MAYITO: Some of us are not born with perfect chemical balance—I have to have them.

CELIN: You've brought drugs with you.

MAYITO: No. I haven't done drugs for years now. I haven't had to.

MARGARITA: Good.

MAYITO: I have friends who are doctors—this is better than drugs.

CELIN: What are they for?

MAYITO: The red ones anxiety; the orange ones take care of the highs, the lows, that kind of thing. These yellow ones get rid of my obsessive nature.

CELIN: There's a lot wrong with you.

MAYITO: Not really. I just don't want to take any chances. The café is very good. Did you do it the old fashioned way?

MARGARITA: The old fashioned way? There hasn't been a new way of doing things here for half a century.

(They drink café.)

MAYITO: It's perfect. This whole thing—everything is perfect.

(A pig is slaughtered off stage. The cries of the terrified animal are heard every few moments.)

MAYITO: What is that?

MARGARITA: Oh, God.

MAYITO: What?

MARGARITA: Señor Alberto. He's slaughtering it.

MAYITO: Are you sure?

MARGARITA: Why would he—

CELIN: It does sound—

MARGARITA: Terrible.

CELIN: Awful.

MAYITO: Why is it so loud?

CELIN: If they were gutting you...

MAYITO: Can't you do something?

MARGARITA: I was promised he wouldn't hurt him.

CELIN: You were?

MARGARITA: Yesterday after lunch I brought over the leftovers. I had this feeling in my stomach that he was going to slaughter it soon. The way he didn't look at

me in the eyes. Just took the food and walked away.
I asked him if he was—he said no.

CELIN: We're getting worked up over nothing. He can
do whatever he wants with this...this.... It's his to do
with as he wishes.

MARGARITA: He promised—

CELIN: Didn't want to hurt you.

MARGARITA: I didn't even get to say goodbye. Ever
since you left I make it a point to say goodbye to
everything. I didn't know then you'd be gone forever.

MAYITO: I came back.

MARGARITA: I should have said goodbye to you. That
was cruel of me.

MAYITO: It's over.

MARGARITA: I should have gone to the airport to say
goodbye. Do you forgive me?

MAYITO: Margarita.

MARGARITA: Say you do.

MAYITO: That's so long ago now.

MARGARITA: Say you do.

CELIN: I don't hear it anymore.

(Short pause)

*(*MARGARITA *snaps out of it almost as if nothing had
occurred.)*

MARGARITA: Can I get you more café?

MAYITO: I'm okay.

MARGARITA: And you?

CELIN: No.

MAYITO: Why don't you just take two of these.

MARGARITA: There. I'm over it. All right. You don't have to look at me—don't look at me.

CELIN: Where were you?

MARGARITA: What?

CELIN: This morning.

MARGARITA: I told you.

CELIN: You were lying.

MARGARITA: I was—

CELIN: Lying. Where were you?

MARGARITA: Mayito.

MAYITO: We want to know.

MARGARITA: I'm not in trouble.

MAYITO: Trouble?

CELIN: What are you doing going out so early—

MARGARITA: I don't want you to worry about me.

CELIN: Just tell us—

MARGARITA: I have to clean these.

CELIN: Margarita.

MARGARITA: Margarita nothing. *(She exits.)*

MAYITO: Something is wrong.

CELIN: We'll see tonight.

MAYITO: What?

CELIN: When we follow her. We'll see where she goes.

MAYITO: One day back and I'm already part of the intrigue.

CELIN: You're not part of anything. This isn't your country anymore.

MAYITO: You're probably right.

CELIN: I am right.

(Pause)

MAYITO: What am I?

CELIN: Yes?

MAYITO: You're successful here.

CELIN: Very successful.

MAYITO: Okay. Very successful.

CELIN: Why did you smile when you said that?

MAYITO: It's just...frankly, the successful person never has to say—

CELIN: Oh, fuck off.

MAYITO: I'm just making an observation.

CELIN: Observe yourself. All right?

(Pause)

MAYITO: Okay. You're successful. I agree—
I understand that for you to feel that you have some worth, you have to make me feel—

CELIN: What's your problem?

MAYITO: I just want to know where I stand here?

CELIN: Another worm who left.

MAYITO: My politics forced me to go.

CELIN: You were ten.

MAYITO: Okay. So. I had strong political beliefs.

CELIN: What were they?

(Pause)

MAYITO: I can't remember.

CELIN: There.

MAYITO: There what.

CELIN: Nothing has any lasting significance to you—not then, not now.

MAYITO: Are you still the same person you once were?

CELIN: Of course.

MAYITO: You haven't changed?

CELIN: No. Not one bit.

MAYITO: Arrested development.

CELIN: Huh?

MAYITO: You're stuck in one part of your life—

CELIN: I know what it is.

MAYITO: Freud. Haven't you read Freud?

CELIN: We're not psychological.

MAYITO: You're Marxists?

CELIN: Yes.

MAYITO: I don't think so. I've thought this through—I've been in analysis and I've discovered certain things about you.

CELIN: You go to analysis to discover things about me?

MAYITO: One of us has to.

CELIN: Don't do me any favors.

MAYITO: You stayed behind because—I'm not going to say it.

CELIN: Say it!

MAYITO: No!

CELIN: Just say it!

MAYITO: You were sexually compelled to.

CELIN: What?

MAYITO: You wanted to be close to our mother. There's a psychological time bomb waiting to explode.

CELIN: You're way out of line.

MAYITO: I'm not going to get graphic, but when is it going to hit you that you were sexually attracted to her?

CELIN: Are you nuts? Then if that's true you left because you wanted our father—

MAYITO: To love me. Yes. That's it.

CELIN: To love you?

MAYITO: That's all I ever wanted from him.

CELIN: Have you told your wife this?

MAYITO: Of course. We have sessions together. My wife and I. And the shrink. Once a week.

CELIN: To discuss our father?

MAYITO: Yes. His pull—his effect on my decisions from the kind of books I write to the color of my car.

CELIN: What color is your car?

MAYITO: Mother of pearl; but really I prefer not to discuss that.

CELIN: And now that he's dead your shrink is out of business.

MAYITO: No. Now I go there three times a week. It's even more difficult because there is no one to—my anger has no place to go except.... I'm getting a divorce. Very friendly.

CELIN: What does that mean?

MAYITO: It's *very* friendly.

CELIN: Huh?

MAYITO: We still fuck. Once or twice a week—it's better than it's ever been.

CELIN: How are the kids?

MAYITO: What kids?

CELIN: Your kids.

MAYITO: My kids?

CELIN: Yes. You're getting a divorce, how are they? You do think about the kids?

MAYITO: Well, we get them a sitter, of course. I mean, they don't see us together anymore. Is that what you're asking? If they saw us getting together for sex—

CELIN: That's not what I'm—how are they adjusting to the divorce?

MAYITO: Oh, they're fine. We got them their own shrink. They go almost every day after school.

CELIN: That's what your life is, huh? Going to the shrink—getting his okay on things. I bet you he was the one who told you to come here.

MAYITO: To put closure.

CELIN: What the fuck does closure mean?

MAYITO: If it weren't for him I would have killed my wife and my little brats a long time ago.

CELIN: What?

MAYITO: Forget what I just said. *(He pops some more pills.)* Where did she go? Should I go find her?

CELIN: Are you all right?

MAYITO: Do you care?

CELIN: We have our share of differences. Just understand that.

MAYITO: Yes. Marxism 101.

CELIN: Everything comes down to those who have and those who have not.

MAYITO: Certainly all of your books do. It's frightening what passes for talent in this country.

(Pause)

CELIN: You've read them?

MAYITO: They're better than valium. Are you sure you even write them? Everything in them is what the government wants you to say.

CELIN: Have you read all of them?

MAYITO: Sure.

CELIN: Of course you have. You wouldn't know what to write about if you didn't.

MAYITO: What?

CELIN: The first time I read a book of yours there it was—thief!

MAYITO: Are you kidding me?

CELIN: In your last book you had a boy with no legs—something I wrote about years ago.

MAYITO: It's a metaphor for the exile condition.

CELIN: I know what the metaphor is—I invented it! And the same thing with the blind, that deaf kid—

MAYITO: What about them?

CELIN: Mostly children.

MAYITO: Look; I'm interested in what happens in a young man's life—those first fifteen years or so—

CELIN: *(Overlapping)* You're not listening to me. You're not fucking talking to some reviewer here—you're talking to your own brother, the man you stole your good ideas from.

MAYITO: —I'm intereted in the people around him—
what kind of environment—oh, fuck yourself.

CELIN: Is it just coincidence you write about the same
things I'm interested in?

MAYITO: Maybe. You don't see me getting all—hey,
what's to stop you from looking at my work and—
how do I know you haven't stolen from my—

CELIN: Frankly because it sucks.

MAYITO: Hey!

CELIN: I just want you to admit—

MAYITO: That we both write about this place. There are
bound to be similarities—

CELIN: There's nothing real in your work. You left too
long ago to understand it all. And those moments—
rare moments—that are true are stolen from my work.

MAYITO: We grew up together.

CELIN: Thief!

MAYITO: The memories—oh, don't call me.... The
memories are bound to be similar.

CELIN: What memories? What do you remember?

(Pause)

MAYITO: Nothing.

CELIN: What?

MAYITO: I don't remember anything. I asked the doctor
for some kind of memory pill—something that would
give me back what I've lost. He said, "Are you mad?
Go back home and get it." But already so much has
changed—things are changing right in front of me.
I'm running out of time.

CELIN: We don't have it.

MAYITO: What?

CELIN: Our childhood. It's lost.

MAYITO: The way they split us apart. I want it all back.

CELIN: Every book I've written—

MAYITO: Every word I've written—

CELIN: To get it back.

(Short pause)

MAYITO: I haven't been able to.

CELIN: You haven't?

MAYITO: No.

CELIN: Neither have I.

MAYITO: All those books I've written up to now—
not even close to what I know is the truth. When I
got here—today—this morning in fact—I woke up
and started writing. Finally I understand. This is my
last chance—coming home now is my last chance to
get our childhood down on paper.

CELIN: I stayed and I haven't been able to do that.

MAYITO: You're not as good a writer. Not that it's your
fault. Your childhood is no different from your life now
because you've always been here. My childhood was
taken away so quickly that all that was left for me to do
was try to remember. I travel back and forth, choosing
sometimes home and sometimes New York. To be a
writer is to have two worlds to jump between, each
giving meaning to the other. But you have only the one
and that's death for a writer.

(Short pause)

CELIN: I don't like you. I thought I would. But after all
these years—I don't like you. I liked you then. When
we were kids. I don't like you now.

MAYITO: What are you going to do about it?

(Short pause)

CELIN: So that's it over there. What you were writing this morning? The new novel?

MAYITO: Yes.

CELIN: You didn't want me to read it because—

MAYITO: I don't want you stealing what I have.

CELIN: You coming home—you're the thief. I stayed.

MAYITO: So what?

CELIN: It's the one thing I have. No I'm not fucking friends with Clint Eastwood. I don't have a shrink or all this medication, I don't have a fancy car, but I have a solid sense of my past. I'm claiming it and you're not going to take it.

MAYITO: What are you doing?

CELIN: You're not going to steal what I have.

MAYITO: Let go of that.

(CELIN takes out the sheet from the typewriter. He rips it in half.)

CELIN: Not today.

(MARGARITA enters with the bloody head of a pig.)

MARGARITA: I stole it.

CELIN: What?

MARGARITA: I went next door and stole it.

CELIN: What did you do that for?

MARGARITA: I didn't get a chance to say goodbye.

(Blackout)

END OF ACT ONE

ACT TWO

Scene One

(A day later)

(CELIN is on stage holding a letter. MAYITO is there watching him. After a moment, CELIN reads from the letter.)

CELIN: "Today I received a final rejection. It was for a book I wrote soon after arriving. I remember the first few letters—polite, appreciative, kind even—but none of them would give me the time of day. Somehow—no, not somehow—the U S Postal system lost this one final letter over twenty years ago and now there it was in front of me. As if there had been this one bullet coming all this time and now it'd finally found it's destination. I'm using a .38 Special with hollow point bullets—

MAYITO: He didn't say hollow point.

CELIN: I'm making it more specific—real. It's a little dull right now.

MAYITO: Please don't rewrite our father's suicide note.

(CELIN returns to reading.)

CELIN: "As far as demands, don't take me back to that stinking pit of an island. Leave me at some airport, perhaps I'll end up somewhere different. Oh, dear, can hear Ellsie upstairs. There is no space in this country. I bet this one shot will shut Ellsie up for a while. I best get on with it before she drives me mad. One last thing.

There is one book I left behind. It's buried somewhere in the house. You find it it's yours. Everyone would agree that it's a work of extraordinary power."

(CELIN *looks at* MAYITO.)

CELIN: You think our dad was fucking Ellsie?

MAYITO: You went through my stuff.

CELIN *looks at the letter again.*

CELIN: "As if there had been this one bullet coming all this time and now it'd finally found it's destination."

(Blackout)

Scene Two

(A day later)

(The study)

(CELIN *is searching through drawers in the desk.* MARGARITA *enters. He is startled.*)

MARGARITA: What are you doing?

CELIN: Nothing.

MARGARITA: That didn't look like nothing. What were you looking for?

(CELIN *checks that* MAYITO *is not listening.*)

CELIN: Whom do you like better? Mayito or me.

MARGARITA: I like you both the same.

CELIN: Oh, come on.

MARGARITA: No, really.

CELIN: You mean you don't like either one of us.

MARGARITA: If that's what I meant—

CELIN: What don't you like about me? Our brother I understand—there's so little to like but what about—

MARGARITA: You are heartless—not that he's any better. The both of you—

CELIN: All this anger of yours is going to catch up with you.

MARGARITA: Mayito said the same thing to me last night. I don't know what you two are talking about.

CELIN: I want to be a better brother—not the kind that only comes home for funerals.

MARGARITA: I'm thinking of letting go of this house.

CELIN: Why?

MARGARITA: It's too big. The government has come around. They want to build a school. I told them I'd think about it.

CELIN: You can't! I mean you could—if you wanted to, but why would you? This is all we have left of our parents. Of ourselves really.

MARGARITA: The only reason you come back now is because of this house—this structure.

CELIN: I come home because of you. The house has no sentimental value.

MARGARITA: Then why don't you want me to get rid of it?

CELIN: This is ours. Forget sentimentality. It goes way beyond that. It's ours and you don't go and throw away what's ours.

MARGARITA: I can't stand having to keep this alive for both of you.

CELIN: Ah. There it is. I heard anger.

MARGARITA: No.

CELIN: Yes.

MARGARITA: If you were looking for the gun I keep it in the bedroom now.

CELIN: The gun?

MARGARITA: Yes. So go.

CELIN: What's it doing in the bedroom?

MARGARITA: What's it doing so near my bed? That's what you want to ask me?

CELIN: Margarita.

MARGARITA: If a thief were to break in I'd have a way to defend myself.

CELIN: But you're not going to—

MARGARITA: Shoot myself? No. Why would I?

CELIN: This family does have—

MARGARITA: Do you want to kill yourself?

CELIN: Sometimes. Not seriously.

MARGARITA: How then?

CELIN: I don't know. It's the kind of thing one watches in movies or reads about in old novels. It's never messy, of course. I'm afraid to be messy.

MARGARITA: So you do think about it?

CELIN: The way I think about sex.

MARGARITA: How do you think about sex?

CELIN: It's this constant thing. Look, you're my sister and the last person I'm going to talk about sex to.

MARGARITA: I've never done it.

CELIN: What?

MARGARITA: I know it seems impossible.

CELIN: Never? Forget the reference point then.

MARGARITA: No. Never.

CELIN: Well, okay, okay, that's...okay. I guess. It's not that big a deal.

MARGARITA: But you constantly think about it.

CELIN: Well, it's a big deal to me.

MARGARITA: Why?

CELIN: It's the only time I feel perfectly adequate. Look, I can't write anymore. I start something and I can't get past page six. This happens more often nowadays. I have writer's block, which means I'm having more and more sex to compensate. And it's good for a while. Really good. I mean terrific, but what I really want is to write a new book.

MARGARITA: I just read your new book.

CELIN: Something I wrote years ago—not good enough then, but I had to give them something.

MARGARITA: I couldn't tell the difference.

CELIN: Who asked you?! That's not the point anyway.

MARGARITA: I'm sorry.

CELIN: For two years now. Not a word.

MARGARITA: So this has made you suicidal.

CELIN: Our brother has made me suicidal. I heard him typing up a storm last night in his room. He's writing a novel about our childhood.

MARGARITA: About the three of us?

CELIN: Two days and he's already stealing.

MARGARITA: What?

CELIN: Nothing here belongs to him. He left it all behind when he chose to leave. Look at all these reviews. *(He takes out a whole bunch of papers from his pocket.)*

MARGARITA: You know I don't read—

CELIN: Translation is on the other side.

MARGARITA: These are all about Mayito. *(She looks them over.)*

CELIN: His writing—according to critics—has only gotten worse from one novel to the next. Did you know that? The attention to detail—situation—not the same as it once was.

MARGARITA: Where did you get these?

CELIN: Our Writer's Union. They keep files on writers living abroad.

MARGARITA: You spy on our brother?

CELIN: *They* do. Yes. I'm only using their resources.

MARGARITA: I don't care what you call it. It's still spying.

CELIN: That's not the point. Look at this. His last book. They didn't just say it was bad. They said it read like a work in progress.

MARGARITA: You once told me never to believe reviews.

CELIN: I did say that, but only when they were about me—and only when they were negative. People have trouble understanding good political...never mind. Our brother is an opportunist. He thinks that by coming back they—the critical establishment— the Public—will start to take him seriously again. I'm not going to let him use us.

MARGARITA: Is that why you wanted the gun?

CELIN: No. Of course not. I was hoping I'd find his new book. He has no right to come here and use us for some novel then just take off.

MARGARITA: You thought he'd leave it out here?

CELIN: I was hoping.

MARGARITA: He wouldn't be so careless.

(CELIN *stops looking for a moment.*)

CELIN: Love me.

MARGARITA: What?

CELIN: I want you to tell me that you love more than him.

MARGARITA: Why are you—

CELIN: I saw this American film once. This woman— she had to make a choice. If you had to make a choice.

MARGARITA: What are you talking about?

CELIN: One would live; one would die. If you had to make that choice. There she was with her two children and only one would live. The other one would be taken from her. It's typical American melodrama but I was bawling because at some point in our lives...at some point someone chose.... I can't keep lying—all this crap about choosing to stay because I believed in this thing, Marxism—they chose for us. We have been lying to ourselves. They chose who went, who stayed. So now I'm just asking you to choose me—do what my father never did. Would you please—

MARGARITA: That last day we were together I disappeared. They still hadn't decided what to do about me or so I thought. Anyway, I hid there under the desk. I said, if they find me I'll tell them I want to go, but if they don't.... I don't think he even came looking for me.

CELIN: We have to stick together. Look; I want to move back in.

MARGARITA: You do?

CELIN: Just for a while. As if I had never left. I want to write again. I think I can get some work done here. I've had enough sex.

MARGARITA: And your wife?

CELIN: She's had enough sex. This is all there is for me now.

MARGARITA: Writing?

CELIN: I was happy once. Let me come home. I want to be happy again.

MARGARITA: Now? After all these years you want to move back in.

CELIN: I'll go get fresh bread every day—

MARGARITA: What?

CELIN: To the other side of town. That old bakery you like. The man—remember the man with the birthmark on the side of his—it's a half hour walk but if you let me—

MARGARITA: Miguel?

CELIN: Yes! That's his name.

MARGARITA: He died years ago, Celin.

(Pause)

CELIN: Oh. People die, don't they?

MARGARITA: Yes. Particularly when you're not paying attention.

CELIN: I need to come home.

(CELIN *hugs* MARGARITA.)

(MAYITO *enters with a camera. He takes a photograph of* CELIN *and* MARGARITA.)

MARGARITA: Where were you?

MAYITO: I went walking. Shooting. I wanted to take some photographs—what I remembered. Not much left. Several of the old buildings are charred now. Sad really. I walked over to the ice cream stand on Olivio and that burned down the night I got here.

CELIN: When are you going back to New York?

(MARGARITA *starts to exit.*)

MAYITO: Good news. Hey, where are you going?

MARGARITA: I have something to do.

MAYITO: You don't want to hear the good news?

MARGARITA: You've decided to stay.

MAYITO: Yes! Yes...at least for... Are you happy?

MARGARITA: Yes.

MAYITO: You don't look happy. Are your wrists okay?

(MAYITO *looks at* MARGARITA's *wrists.*)

MARGARITA: Fine.

MAYITO: They were a little too rough with you.

MARGARITA: I'm all right.

CELIN: If I weren't here you'd still be in jail.

MAYITO: If I hadn't flashed some cold hard American cash, who knows when they would have let you go.

MARGARITA: Thank you—both of you.

MAYITO: What gave you the crazy idea of stealing the head of that—Señor Alberto.

MARGARITA: I felt like it.

MAYITO: Why?

MARGARITA: Ever since you both got here you've been asking why. Why am I this way? Why do I act like this?

MAYITO: We're concerned.

MARGARITA: And what happens when you go away? You know, people are always leaving me and I seem to be okay. So thank you both, but please, do what you have to do and get out soon. (*She exits.*)

(*Pause*)

MAYITO: Look; you mind?

CELIN: What?

MAYITO: I want to do some more work on my new book.

CELIN: I'm staying too.

MAYITO: Good. So why don't you go stay in the other room.

CELIN: This is as much mine as it is yours.

(MARGARITA *enters with a gun.*)

MAYITO: What the fuck are you doing?

MARGARITA: You never saw it—a relic from the past. Why don't you take a picture of it?

MAYITO: Is that it—is that the one she used. Oh, Jesus! Do you know what you're doing with that?

MARGARITA: I think so.

MAYITO: Is it—it's not loaded, is it?

MARGARITA: What good would it do me if it weren't?

MAYITO: Don't—you know you should never point a gun at anyone.

MARGARITA: You're so smart.

MAYITO: Stop smiling.

MARGARITA: I'm giving this to him.

(MARGARITA *hands* CELIN *the gun.*)

CELIN: Why?

MARGARITA: In case a thief were to break in. What would I do with it?

CELIN: It's heavy.

MAYITO: It's a gun.

CELIN: This new novel of yours—

MAYITO: Would you put that down.

CELIN: How much is it worth to you?

MAYITO: What?

CELIN: How much are they paying you to write it?

MAYITO: I guess—it's not the amount that's important—

CELIN: What the fuck does that mean?

MAYITO: I'm just saying numbers don't tell the whole story.

CELIN: I don't want the whole story. I just want to know how much you're getting paid.

MARGARITA: How much are you selling yourself for?

MAYITO: Oh, okay, I see—brother and sister bonding.

CELIN: How much?

MAYITO: I got a...hundred...thousand.

CELIN: How much?!

MAYITO: You have to understand, in New York the standard of living...it's a bit different.

CELIN: I'd say so.

MARGARITA: It's only been fired once.

(CELIN *looks over at* MARGARITA.)

CELIN: What did you say?

MARGARITA: Only once.

MAYITO: Yes. And it's not going to be fired—

(CELIN *cocks the gun.*)

MAYITO: Are you crazy?

CELIN: I heard you typing last night.

MAYITO: I did do some work.

CELIN: With his typewriter.

MAYITO: Yes. I brought it into my room and used it.

CELIN: Don't move it again.

MAYITO: Why?

CELIN: I don't want you taking it out of this room. It's always been here. That's where it'll stay.

MAYITO: Who cares—

CELIN: I do.

MARGARITA: If you want to work on your book it looks like you're going to have to do it in here.

(MAYITO *exits.*)

CELIN: Thank you.

MARGARITA: Why?

CELIN: The gun.

MARGARITA: Oh.

CELIN: It scared him.

MARGARITA: I saw you following me last night.

CELIN: I wanted to know—

MARGARITA: You were so obvious.

CELIN: Where do you go at night?

MARGARITA: None of your business. *(She turns to go.)*

CELIN: We can get through this together.

MARGARITA: Through what?

CELIN: Our brother. He'll finish his book, he'll go away.

MARGARITA: You both will.

CELIN: You chose me today. That means a lot to me.

MARGARITA: I guess you can look at it that way.

CELIN: What do you mean?

MARGARITA: I don't know what I'm hoping for more. For you to shoot him or to shoot yourself. *(She exits.)*

(CELIN puts the gun to his head. He holds it there for a moment.)

(And then almost under his breath...)

CELIN: Too messy.

(Blackout)

Scene Three

(Two weeks later)

(MAYITO is working at the typewriter. Offstage we hear all sorts of banging and things falling, as if there's construction going on.)

(CELIN enters with a pick and starts to tear the floor apart.)

MAYITO: No luck?

CELIN: I think I'm getting close to finding it.

MAYITO: You're going to have to put this house back in order before we go.

CELIN: I know.

MAYITO: What are you going to do about all the holes in the livingroom?

CELIN: I'll figure something out.

MAYITO: This house looks like shit.

CELIN: I'll worry about the house when I find Papi's extraordinary book.

MAYITO: Extraodinary—and you believe him?

CELIN: You wouldn't be back if you didn't.

MAYITO: I'm not back for a book that may or may not exist.

CELIN: I'm sure you're not.

MAYITO: It's our book.You find it, it's ours.

CELIN: You keep saying it doesn't really exist but then you keep insisting I share it with you.

MAYITO: I'm just saying—

CELIN: It's mine.

(MAYITO *rises;* CELIN *picks up the pick. A moment of confrontation before* MAYITO *backs down. They return to working. After a moment,* CELIN *cuts himself.)*

CELIN: Shit. Fuck.

MAYITO: Are you okay?

CELIN: I hate him for making me do this. *(Pause)* When was the last time you spoke to him?

MAYITO: Every few months he'd have me over to read to him from his work—the work he'd done before he left this country.

CELIN: Why?

MAYITO: He was going blind and he wanted to know the sum of his life. I felt sorry for the old man, but one day by his bed I saw a copy of some new book he'd been reading. He wasn't blind after all. Just wanted to make sure I understood I was only half the writer he was.

CELIN: What did you say to him?

MAYITO: Fuck you asshole.

CELIN: What?

MAYITO: Nothing. I said nothing. Instead, I read to him that night but more than that, I listened. To his words. The old man was a good writer. What was I going to say? I ripped a page out when he wasn't looking. Afterwards I called my wife. We were already separated. I read it to her and told her I'd written it. I wanted her to know just how good I was. My wife left me for another writer—a food critic with a perfect body, which doesn't make sense. On top of that he knows several languages, loves to go riding and she told me all these things the night we decided to separate as if to say, when you've done all those things come back and then we'll talk.

CELIN: You mentioned that you still have sex with your wife?

MAYITO: I have sex with myself and I imagine her there, so I'm not sure what you'd call that.

CELIN: I'd call that disturbing.

(MAYITO *starts to work again. This time really banging on the keys. After a moment* MARGARITA *enters.*)

MARGARITA: I've written a poem.

CELIN: Don't you think we have enough writers in this family?!

(Pause)

(CELIN *and* MAYITO *return to work.*)

MARGARITA: What have you done to the floor?

MAYITO: He did it.

CELIN: I'll put it back together again. I'll get this whole house straightened.

MARGARITA: I don't care what happens to this house.

CELIN: Shortly before leaving Papi buried some book of his somewhere in this place.

MARGARITA: Oh.

MAYITO: It's his best work.

MARGARITA: Can I read you my poem?

MAYITO: Why don't you get married?

MARGARITA: Why do I need to get married?

MAYITO: At some point or other, we must all get old and marriage is the easiest way to get there.

MARGARITA: You're both married and you act like children.

MAYITO: I'm separated.

CELIN: I refuse to get old.

MAYITO: I'm worried about you. What's going to happen when we leave?

MARGARITA: It isn't as if you haven't done it before.

MAYITO: What'll you do?

MARGARITA: When you're around you don't pay me much attention. No different when you're gone.

CELIN: We're busy.

MARGARITA: Yes. I know.

MAYITO: I don't know where the time goes. I've been—

MARGARITA: In your own world.

MAYITO: The world we used to live in.

MARGARITA: Am I there? Am I in that world with you?

(MAYITO *gets up and looks at* MARGARITA.)

MAYITO: You have my attention. What do you want to say to me? Go ahead.

MARGARITA: Can I read my poem?

CELIN: Writing has only made us unhappy.

MARGARITA: Mayito?

MAYITO: He's right.

MARGARITA: I thought exile had made you unhappy.

MAYITO: That too.

MARGARITA: And your marriage?

MAYITO: I'm an unhappy man. What can I say.

CELIN: He doesn't want you to get hurt.

MARGARITA: I have talent.

CELIN: You make the best café.

MARGARITA: Is that it? I do other things.

MAYITO: Of course you do—the way you fold our clothes—

MARGARITA: It's just I've never been allowed to express myself.

MAYITO: Now that's just silly. Who's saying no to you?

CELIN: Do you mind getting me a glass of water?

(MARGARITA *starts to walk away.*)

MAYITO: What is it that you need to say that you have to submit yourself to this awful life?

(CELIN *is working on his own.*)

MARGARITA: I write about home. A home with both of you in it - with all of us. A home that includes me—

when we were little. We were happy. The three of us and we would put on plays and write stories. And it didn't matter that Celin was Wendy and I was a boy or that—

CELIN: *I was never Wendy!*

MARGARITA: We were friends.

MAYITO: We're still friends.

MARGARITA: You look at me differently.

MAYITO: What?

MARGARITA: Like someone from your past but that's just it, I'm here now. Living here now. I'm not a ghost wandering through this house. When was the last time we sat down and talked. Instead, you're locked in here half the time trying to get back something that's long gone. Pay attention to what remains before you lose that too. *(She exits.)*

CELIN: You need to sneak some more of your pills into her food.

MAYITO: I've run out of them.

CELIN: What's going to happen to her?

MAYITO: What's going to happen to me?

(Outside, thunder is heard.)

MAYITO: I can't fucking do this with all the commotion. *(Pause)* On the way here when I first caught sight of the island I threw up.

CELIN: That's gross.

MAYITO: Yes. Yes it is. It's fucking the ugly side of America just coming up on me.

CELIN: No. It's just gross.

MAYITO: Confronted with the reality of what this country really is—I mean there it was. I could just stretch my hand out and grab it.

CELIN: You're so possesive.

MAYITO: What do you mean?

CELIN: Everything is about grabbing, owning—

MAYITO: No. It was different. It was this terrible fear that everything I've dedicated my life to—that I could be wrong all across the board—my family, my writing... my country. Here I was about to be confronted with the evidence. I was about to learn just how limited my vision was.

(Pause)

CELIN: Hey, Mayito?

MAYITO: What?

CELIN: What's it like to make money—

MAYITO: I don't think about it.

CELIN: —to put a value on things.

MAYITO: It comes naturally.

CELIN: Do you own a vacuum cleaner?

MAYITO: A vacuum cleaner—the height of luxury, huh? You have no idea how we live.

CELIN: No. Not really.

MAYITO: I don't own one.

CELIN: So you're not that rich.

MAYITO: I pay someone to come clean my house.

CELIN: A maid?

MAYITO: It sounds awful, doesn't it? To just call her that.

CELIN: Isn't that what she is?

MAYITO: I don't know. Things are in flux right now. I'm fucking her so I don't know what to call her. That's not true. I call her plenty of things, none of which I'm going to tell you.

CELIN: Fucking the proletariat, huh?

MAYITO: Yeah. Come to think of it. That's what I do. I fuck the proletariat.

CELIN: So does she still clean your house?

MAYITO: It wouldn't really be fucking the proletariat if she didn't.

CELIN: Do you like your life—do you like money?

MAYITO: I hate my life. I love money. Does that answer your question?

CELIN: Why don't you continue writing—I'll be really quiet.

MAYITO: Why?

CELIN: Isn't that what you want?

MAYITO: Why are you being so nice all of a sudden?

(CELIN *and* MAYITO *work.*)

(MAYITO *looks up at the leaky roof.*)

MAYITO: That's driving me nuts.

CELIN: He's pissing on us. Did he stop loving you?

MAYITO: I'm not sure he ever did. The man only loved himself.

CELIN: He had his favorite.

MAYITO: When my first book was published I gave him a copy. He didn't read it—well he doesn't read English, but I wanted him to say something, anything. Congratulations. About a week later I saw some homeless man selling it on the corner of his building.

There it was. It had my autograph and what I'd written to him. I bought it back for a dollar. I still have it. I stopped giving him my books after that. As soon as one got published I'd leave it in front of his door.

CELIN: He didn't know it was you?

MAYITO: Of course he fucking knew but I wanted him to never forget I was a writer—a successful one. I was nothing like him. Nothing.

CELIN: He sent them to me. I thought it was you trying to rub it in my face.

MAYITO: He sent them to you?

CELIN: With no note. Nothing. Just the books. Your address of course. As if they were coming from you. All of them with that stupid grin of yours in the back.

MAYITO: That photograph is by Annie Liebowitz.

CELIN: Liebo who?

MAYITO: Famous photographer.

CELIN: It doesn't mean she's any good. You look like you're posing.

MAYITO: I am.

CELIN: You look like a prick.

MAYITO: Fuck off.

CELIN: I wanted to kill you. For rubbing it in. I could have taken a knife and...and...but luckily for you I am not a violent man.

MAYITO: Luckily for me you can't get a visa out of this hellhole.

CELIN: I'm getting sick of you.

(MARGARITA *enters with a glass of water.*)

CELIN: You didn't put any ice in this.

(MARGARITA *exits.*)

(*After a moment* CELIN *and* MAYITO *return to work.*)

CELIN: Mayito.

MAYITO: What?

CELIN: I want a yacht.

MAYITO: What are you talking about?

CELIN: It's just...it would be a nice thing...it's a nice idea.

MAYITO: A yacht?

CELIN: Sure. If you have enough money—that thing you're writing. If you're willing to share—

MAYITO: I never have enough money. No one ever has enough money.

(MARGARITA *enters and hands* CELIN *the glass of water.*)

MARGARITA: Anything else? Mayito?

MAYITO: What?

MARGARITA: Would you like anything?

(MAYITO *doesn't even bother answering her.*)

CELIN: Let him write.

MAYITO: Why are *you* so interested in what I'm doing?

CELIN: There are many ways to handle a thief. If you can get him to work for you.

MAYITO: What are you talking about?

(MARGARITA *exits.*)

CELIN: Just start writing.

MAYITO: You can't tell me what to do.

CELIN: I can suggest.

MAYITO: You're not suggesting. You're telling me.

CELIN: Where did she go?

MAYITO: I don't know.

CELIN: She was just here.

MAYITO: She drifts. Have you noticed that?

(Blackout)

Scene Four

(Two weeks later)

(A fire engine is heard in the darkness.)

(Lights come up on MAYITO *staring at the typewriter.* CELIN *watches him. They are both in underwear and T-shirts, and look like they haven't gotten any rest. The floor is littered with paper airplanes.)*

(The room is a real mess.)

MAYITO: Stop watching me.

CELIN: Are you almost done?

MAYITO: Yes.

*(*MAYITO *goes back to typing.* CELIN *makes a paper airplane. Another fire engine goes by.)*

CELIN: There goes another one. They're coming from all over to fight the fires.

MAYITO: I don't care.

CELIN: The whole town is on fire.

MAYITO: Shut up.

CELIN: Aren't you sad? I mean, isn't that why you're here. For your town—your past.

MAYITO: It's all here. I don't have to have the real thing.

(MAYITO *points to a stack of papers next to him.*
He continues to type. CELIN *throws the paper airplane.*
It flies around the stage. The brothers stop to look at it.
The plane crashes.)

MAYITO: Don't do that again.

CELIN: Why?

MAYITO: It's distracting.

CELIN: What am I supposed to do?

MAYITO: This is ridiculous. I'm taking the typewriter
into the other room.

CELIN: Don't. *(He picks up the gun that has sat unnoticed*
on the desk.)

MAYITO: You want me to finish this?

CELIN: Yes.

MAYITO: Then you're going to have to sit there and
not say anything.

CELIN: Shhh. *(He types.)*

(A fire engine drives by.)

MAYITO: *Shut up!*

CELIN: Let me get you a shot of rum.

*(*MAYITO *types.)*

CELIN: You look like shit.

MAYITO: So do you.

*(*CELIN *drinks.)*

CELIN: What's his name. Gorba—Gorbochef. Gorbachef.
Fuck. They go through so many of them how are we
supposed to keep up with pronunciations. How long
do you think he's going to last?

MAYITO: Forever. He's young.

CELIN: You know what the first—one of the first things he did. He tells the Soviets to stop drinking. As if that will ever happen.

MAYITO: I'm trying to finish this.

(Pause)

CELIN: Are you almost done?

MAYITO: Almost. Just keep yourself busy over there.

CELIN: I can't wait to read it. Our new novel. Let me type The End on it.

MAYITO: You can do whatever the hell you want.

CELIN: A first. You write it but we both get credit for it.

MAYITO: In New York that's standard practice.

CELIN: Really?

MAYITO: People take credit for other people's work all the time.

CELIN: I'm not taking credit for anything. It's mine.

MAYITO: Ours.

CELIN: Our childhood.

MAYITO: Yes. Now fuck off so I can finish this.

(CELIN walks over to the hole from the previous scene— it is much larger. He continues to remove tiles making the hole even bigger.)

CELIN: What am I going to do with fifty thousand dollars? *(Short pause)* Go to Switzerland.

MAYITO: What did you say?

CELIN: I have this incredible appetite for blondes and chocolate—blondes in chocolate.

MAYITO: Marxists don't run off to Switzerland.

CELIN: All right. So what. What I really want to do is fuck the proletariat for a while. I want to know what that feels like.

MAYITO: I can tell you that from personal experience it's no different than fucking a capitalist. There are, of course, some variations but aren't there always?

CELIN: You know what I mean. I don't care anymore. Really.

MAYITO: Why not?

CELIN: It gave me a few books—what more can it give me. I'd rather have you.

MAYITO: You would?

CELIN: A brother is more important than an idea.

MAYITO: All right then, we both go to Switzerland.

CELIN: You mean it? Like brothers.

MAYITO: Would you stop waving that gun around like that.

CELIN: Not competing anymore. We should have done this a long time ago.

MAYITO: Why didn't we?

CELIN: It's not the leaving that hurts. It's knowing there's no chance for a reconciliation. Even in the worst fights there's a chance—people do walk back through the door.

MAYITO: I did come back.

CELIN: I never thought you would.

MAYITO: This politics thing—getting in the way of us. It's not real.

CELIN: The politics?

MAYITO: A way for us to not be vulnerable.

CELIN: Yes. For us to not show how much we were hurt by it all.

MAYITO: I was hurt.

CELIN: I know.

MAYITO: You hurt me.

CELIN: You hurt me.

MAYITO: It's going to be okay.

(CELIN *is very close to* MAYITO.)

MAYITO: Don't hug me though.

CELIN: What?

MAYITO: I'm not there yet. Emotionally, you know. I'm not that fucking sophisticated.

CELIN: What are you talking about?

MAYITO: I have problems with other men showing me affection. I haven't worked up to that moment yet.

CELIN: This is about Papi and your shrink.

MAYITO: Yes.

CELIN: Fuck Papi and fuck your shrink.

(CELIN *hugs* MAYITO. *He kisses him. Not sexual*)

MAYITO: You just kissed me.

CELIN: Yes.

MAYITO: Oh.

CELIN: You can let go now.

MAYITO: I don't want to.

CELIN: It's okay. I'll be here when you let go. I promise.

MAYITO: Okay. Okay. (*He lets go.*)

(*Pause*)

(MAYITO *returns to typing.* CELIN *looks for the father's book.)*

CELIN: I think this is it.

MAYITO: You found it?

CELIN: It's not very big. What do we do?

MAYITO: Open it.

CELIN: You do it.

MAYITO: No, that's all right. You do it.

CELIN: Are you sure?

MAYITO: Wait. What if it's good?

CELIN: What do you mean?

MAYITO: What if it is really better than anything we've written.

CELIN: We trash it.

MAYITO: Really?

CELIN: We have your book. We don't need anything else.

MAYITO: You've been looking for this the whole time.

CELIN: I've been looking for you the whole time. *(He tears the package open.)*

MAYITO: Oh, God!

CELIN: Peter Pan!

MAYITO: What!

(CELIN *and* MAYITO *open the book.)*

CELIN: It is. It's a copy of *Peter Pan.*

MAYITO: Why would he do this?

CELIN: Unless....

MAYITO: Yes?

CELIN: Unless he was nuts.

MAYITO: Our father thought he wrote *Peter Pan*.

CELIN: This is our copy. From when we were kids.

MAYITO: It is?

CELIN: It's got both our names on it. *I was Wendy.*

MAYITO: There's a note. *(He reads the note.)* "I have stopped writing. This country—this government has taken that from me, but will I have it where I'm going? This was the house I was born in—this room was the nursery. Then my playroom. And many years later my office. The book you're holding I gave you when you were boys. It was my copy. I thought the world was easily divided between the real and the Neverland. And if I could only find my way back to the Neverland I would always be able to write. And though the house has changed—there is a garage now where your great grandmother's bedroom was—this remained for me always Neverland. My nursery. My room. My office. I always wondered if it was true that after a while there are parents who lock the bedroom window so their children can't fly back in." *(Pause)* There it is.

CELIN: His voice.

MAYITO: Of course he'd leave his typewriter here. What was left to say?

CELIN: What?

MAYITO: I mean, he wasn't just going to write about all the terrible things happening here.

CELIN: Then he should have stayed—used his talent to help his country.

MAYITO: Lie after lie trying to fool people. He was too good a writer to do that. His only choice really was to stop writing.

CELIN: And the only thing we've done is...

MAYITO: Write. That's it. That's all we've done. Nothing good—nothing of consequence. Just words.... *(He goes back to the typewriter. He sits, silently. After a while he gets up.)*

CELIN: Are you done?

MAYITO: It's good enough. That's been the story of my life.

(CELIN walks over and types The End on it.)

CELIN: I would never have killed you.

MAYITO: That's good to know.

CELIN: No really. I wouldn't have.

MAYITO: I know.

CELIN: Let me read it. *(He picks up the manuscript excited.)* A little long, don't you think. Never mind. *(He sits down to read.)*

(MARGARITA walks in covered completely in soot.)

MAYITO: What's wrong with you?

MARGARITA: I was by the fires. Everything is burning.

MAYITO: You were fighting the fires?

MARGARITA: Yes. There are hundreds of people out there.

MAYITO: Should we go—

CELIN: This is more important.

MARGARITA: What is it?

CELIN: Mayito finished it.

MARGARITA: You finished your book?

CELIN: Our childhood is in here. Ours now—most people never have a chance to get it back.

(MAYITO *takes* MARGARITA *aside.* CELIN *looks through the pages.*)

MAYITO: I feel as if I owe you something.

MARGARITA: What do you mean?

MAYITO: An explanation—some kind of... I've been locked in here writing and haven't really spent a moment alone with you. I'm going to stay a little while longer.

MARGARITA: No you're not.

MAYITO: Yes. Yes I am.

CELIN: We're going to Switzerland.

MARGARITA: Switzerland?

CELIN: She needs to know the truth. He's splitting the money with me since it's half my story.

MARGARITA: What about me? It's my story too.

MAYITO: I can give you—do you like chocolate?

MARGARITA: What?

CELIN: Maybe she likes blondes.

MAYITO: I thought...well, that you could come with us.

MARGARITA: I never left. Why would I leave now.

MAYITO: We'll come back and visit you.

MARGARITA: There's nothing to visit. The town is destroyed. You have nothing to come back to.

MAYITO: This house. You.

MARGARITA: The fire is headed this way.

MAYITO: Should we get out of the way?

CELIN: I'm happy you got it down on paper before it's all destroyed. We have memory now.

MARGARITA: What happens to me in the book?

MAYITO: Actually. Well...a lot happens...that has to do with-

CELIN: You're not in it.

MARGARITA: I'm not?

CELIN: We wanted to make it about brothers. One who left. One who stayed. It's simpler that way.

MAYITO: You would have made things too complicated. You see, I want to make it a movie—a buddy film. If you were in it—three people just doesn't—it's not a buddy film anymore. It's some other kind of film— it's a French film or something.

MARGARITA: What's a buddy film?

MAYITO: It's this homoerotic thing Americans really respond to.

CELIN: Are you saying in this book that me and you— what the fuck are you saying?

MAYITO: You don't understand American film. Do you want to make money?

CELIN: Yes.

MAYITO: Then you're going to have to listen to me.

MARGARITA: What do you believe in, Celin?

CELIN: I believe in my brother's talent. I believe my father is a prick.

MARGARITA: What have you done to him?

MAYITO: Nothing.

MARGARITA: What do the two of you believe in?

CELIN: I can't write anymore. That's all I know.

MAYITO: We're going to write movies. In Switzerland.

CELIN: About brothers who love each other.

MARGARITA: And so you just used home—

CELIN: To get to Switzerland.

(MARGARITA *exits.*)

MAYITO: You didn't have to say that.

CELIN: I wanted to tell her the truth.

MAYITO: I suppose we could take her with us.

CELIN: What can she do?

MAYITO: Does she have to do anything?

CELIN: We have to think about what we want.

MAYITO: I wish Papi were alive. He used to laugh at us.

CELIN: For what?

MAYITO: Just the way we'd fight to prove to the other
we were the real thing. He didn't think either one of
us was any good. Fuck him.

CELIN: We're going to make more money than he ever
dreamed possible. *(He continues to read.)*

(MARGARITA *enters with a small, red tank. It is clearly
labeled gasoline. She begins to pour it all over the room.)*

CELIN: What are you doing? Is that—

MARGARITA: It's water. In case the fires reach here.
Have the whole house watered down.

MAYITO: That's kind of brilliant on your part but it's
not going to help.

MARGARITA: You don't know.

MAYITO: Well, yes, I do know, Margarita.

CELIN: Shh.

MAYITO: He's reading.

MARGARITA: Oh.

MAYITO: Do you think he likes it?

MARGARITA: How do I know?

MAYITO: He's laughing. That's good. That's very good.

MARGARITA: Why don't you ask him?

CELIN: It smells like gasoline in here.

MAYITO: Are you sure that's water?

MARGARITA: It's an old gasoline tank. That's water though.

MAYITO: Wouldn't it be funny if—

MARGARITA: Yeah. It would.

MAYITO: The world.

MARGARITA: What about it?

MAYITO: Ironic.

MARGARITA: There is no irony left in Cuba. Only communism.

MAYITO: No. No. There is. We were fighting a month ago. He and I.

(CELIN *turns the page.*)

MAYITO: Page two.

MARGARITA: He's not laughing anymore.

MAYITO: It's a tragicomedy. *(He takes out a cigarette.)*

MARGARITA: What are you doing?

MAYITO: I'm too nervous—having him read it. I feel so vulnerable.

MARGARITA: This is it.

MAYITO: What?

MARGARITA: Our childhood.

MAYITO: Yeah. He's reading it. *(He searches for his matches.)*

MARGARITA: I'm not even in it.

CELIN: Shhh!

MARGARITA: I want to say goodbye now.

MAYITO: Okay.

MARGARITA: This time I mean. Now.

MAYITO: All right.

MARGARITA: Goodbye. Goodbye, Celin.

CELIN: Shut her up, will you. I'm trying to read.

MAYITO: Do you like it?

CELIN: It's overwritten...but that's okay. It's a first draft.

MAYITO: What?!

CELIN: Just let me concentrate.

MAYITO *goes to strike a match.*

MARGARITA: Goodbye.

MAYITO: Goodbye. There. You feel better.

MARGARITA: Yes.

*(*MAYITO *is about to strike the match.* MARGARITA *closes her eyes and takes a deep breath.)*

MAYITO: What are you doing?

MARGARITA: Nothing.

MAYITO: I think you're crazy.

MARGARITA: I think so too.

MAYITO: Any idea why?

MARGARITA: I think it has something to do with you and him.

MAYITO: With us?

MARGARITA: Yes.

MAYITO: What have we done?

MARGARITA: Nothing.

(MAYITO *goes to strike the match.* MARGARITA *closes her eyes and takes a deep breath.*)

MAYITO: Do you mind me smoking?

MARGARITA: No. Go ahead.

(MAYITO *strikes the match.* MARGARITA *screams. Nothing happens. He isn't able to light it. He tries again. She screams.*)

CELIN: Shhh. I'm reading.

(MAYITO *can't light it.*)

MARGARITA: I'll go get you matches. *(She exits.)*

MAYITO: I think she really is crazy.

CELIN: What? Who?

MAYITO: Our sister. What do you think of the writing now-

CELIN: You use too many words—I just want to get to the fucking ending.

MAYITO: Fuck you.

(MARGARITA *enters.*)

MARGARITA: Here. These work. I tried them already.

MAYITO: Good.

MARGARITA: Can I light it for you?

MAYITO: Sure.

(MARGARITA *goes to light it.*)

MAYITO: Stop.

MARGARITA: What?

MAYITO: I can't smoke. I started drinking again.
I'm going to make movies.

MARGARITA: One cigarette isn't going to destroy you.

MAYITO: Destroy me? That's a little melodramatic,
isn't it?

(*Another fire engine is heard in the distance.*)

MAYITO: They keep coming.

MARGARITA: It's a big fire.

MAYITO: Arsonist.

MARGARITA: Yes.

MAYITO: Margarita, when I was young I got in trouble
for setting Mami's sheets on fire. That wasn't you by
any chance?

MARGARITA: Yes.

MAYITO: Oh, good. I like to clear things up now that
I'm getting on with the rest of my life. (*Pause*) I'm a little
slow but I... If you don't mind me asking, Margarita,
did you start those fires?

MARGARITA: Yes.

MAYITO: It's taken me a little while to put it all—

CELIN: What did you say?

MARGARITA: I started the fires.

MAYITO: And this is gasoline on the floor?

MARGARITA: Yes.

MAYITO: And your intention—what you want is to
blow us all sky high.

MARGARITA: Yes.

MAYITO: Good. I get that now.

CELIN: What the fuck is she talking about?

MAYITO: Our sister is an arsonist.

CELIN: You started those fires?!

MARGARITA: Yes.

CELIN: I don't believe this. And this is all gasoline.

(MARGARITA *holds the matches in her hands.*)

MAYITO: Don't do that.

MARGARITA: Why not?

MAYITO: Why do you want to do this?

MARGARITA: I don't want you to have anywhere to come home to.

CELIN: That doesn't make any—

MAYITO: She's not all there.

MARGARITA: This house. This would be your only place but you're taking it all back with you. I won't ever have you again now that you have your book. I want to destroy it. (*She walks over to where the manuscript is.*)

MAYITO: That's our childhood.

MARGARITA: Yours. Not mine. Papi never saw me. You never saw me. As if I never existed. Now everything— the book and the town will go up in flames. You will never know where you came from. You will try to— you will go to records and accounts but there will be none. Entire city blocks will be razed making room for new ones. And this book—this ugly thing you call your childhood will be no more.

(MARGARITA *sets it on fire. They duck for an explosion but there is none. Only the papers are on fire.*)

CELIN: Are we alive?

MAYITO: No.

CELIN: Yes. Yes. We are. *We're alive.*

(MAYITO *tries to stop the papers from burning but can't.*)

MAYITO: Everything I had worked my whole life for. I had finally done it right.

(MARGARITA *sits to one side.* CELIN *is on the other side.*)

CELIN: What's going to happen now?

MAYITO: What do you mean?

CELIN: Our book? Switzerland. Brothers. Friendship.

MAYITO: How am I going to write now?

CELIN: I will help you.

MAYITO: I have no memory—and this place—look at what we did to this place. I will never know who I am.

CELIN: Will I? It seems my fate is tied to yours. That what I am is the missing part of you—what I was able to give you in that book.

MAYITO: We will never find ourselves again.

CELIN: I know.

MAYITO: I should go. There is nothing here.

CELIN: Will you ever come back?

MAYITO: No.

CELIN: I'm lost. Do you understand. Don't go.

MAYITO: I'm just as lost as you are.

CELIN: Can't we help each other.

MAYITO: It's over. (*He starts to go.*)

MARGARITA: Goodbye.

MAYITO: (*To* CELIN) Goodbye.

(MAYITO *stands in his own light.*)

CELIN: You heard him.

MARGARITA: Yes.

CELIN: You aren't any more lost than we are.

(A gunshot is heard. The light fades on MAYITO.*)*

*(*CELIN *starts to go.)*

MARGARITA: Goodbye.

*(*CELIN *stands in his own light.)*

MARGARITA: The burden has been lifted.

(In the distance another fire engine is heard.)

(A second gunshot is heard. The light fades on CELIN.*)*

(A light on MARGARITA. *Everything burns around her.)*

MARGARITA: If you will just sit there a moment I will
tell you the real story of our childhood. I've been
writing it now for—close to my whole life. I showed
Papi chapter one when I was eight and he marked it up
with red ink and said I couldn't do it. I kept it all inside.
I have it all memorized. My brothers wrote theirs down
and forgot to include me, but they are such a part of
mine. They really loved each other those two. Blindly.
To the point of rage. And I loved them. *(Pause)* If you
will sit there a moment, I will tell you the real story
of our childhood.

(Lights fade slowly.)

END OF PLAY

www.ingramcontent.com/pod-product-compliance
Lightning Source LLC
Chambersburg PA
CBHW052206090426
42741CB00010B/2432